■ SCHOLASTIC

NO BORING PRACTICE, PLEASE!

SPELLING

Reproducible Practice Pages PLUS Easy-to-Score
Quizzes That Reinforce Spelling Rules and Skills

by Harold Jarnicki

New York • Toronto • London • Auckland • Sydney
New Delhi • Mexico City • Hong Kong • Buenos Aires

Teaching *Resources*

Cover by Jaime Lucero
Cover illustrations Mike Moran
Interior design by NEO Grafika
Illustrations by Kelly Kennedy

ISBN 0-439-53149-7
Copyright © 2005 by Harold Jarnicki
All rights reserved.
Printed in the U.S.A.

3 4 5 6 7 8 9 10   40   12 11 10 09 08

Table of Contents

Introduction

magine a classroom where students do not slump in their seats every time you announce it's time for spelling; where spelling lessons and practice bring exciting opportunities along with a couple of laughs and a little competition; where students get emotionally involved in spelling fundamentals, and improvement is proudly displayed by students and recognized by teachers and parents.

You might think such a classroom is merely a figment of my imagination or a fantasy of some ambitiously naive first-year education grad. I can boldly claim that such is not the case. I have been teaching for about 20 years and, with the help of some games, a few jokes, and other gimmicks, have witnessed students get excited about spelling, grammar, vocabulary, and more.

The No Boring Practice, Please! series is an extension of my classroom and one humble step toward helping kids do what comes naturally—learn. If you're ready to add spice to your spelling lessons, then this book is for you.

Carefully structured as a good basic course of study, the recipe for each lesson is simple. *No Boring Practice, Please! Spelling* dishes up straight spelling practice with a dash (or splash) of fun. Inside you'll find a concoction of reproducible pages that cover syllabication, plurals, silent letters, spelling rules (and rule breakers), commonly confused words, and more. Flavored with engaging illustrations and an edgy design, each practice page is easy for kids to swallow. Best of all, you can serve these pages with only a minimal amount of teacher instruction.

Each unit opens with a brief, simple explanation of a key spelling rule or concept in easy-to-understand language. Students are then challenged to apply what they are learning through practice pages, followed by a quick and easy-to-score quiz. Occasionally, you may want to add an extra exercise or practice test depending on students' progress, but the units are designed to stand on their own.

You may wonder what inspired me to write this book—and the rest of the No Boring Practice, Please! series. Let me start at the beginning. As a baby boomer's hyperactive kid, I wasn't a huge fan of school. Sitting at a desk most of the day was tough enough. Add a generous helping of dry spelling rules and my eyes would glaze over, roll back in my head, and send me into a near comatose state where hands on clocks ceased to move.

Years passed. After a less-than-stellar career in rock 'n' roll, I decided the teaching profession was a more lucrative gig. I had two specific goals: (1) to become the teacher I never had; and (2) add a little rock 'n' roll to the school system.

Like it or not, we are teaching a new breed of children—one that watches more than four hours of values-distorting TV each day, plays mindless video games on a regular basis, and gobbles up entertainment far more than nutriment. We welcome these media-savvy kids into our classrooms and expect them to get excited about plurals, silent letters, and syllabication. Let's get real!

This is what drives the No Boring Practice, Please! series. The series is academically sound and rich in language-skill development, but all of its information is disguised by a hip design and comical illustrations that have lots of kid appeal. Think of the series as whole-grain oats packaged in a box of tutti-frutti breakfast cereal.

I know that students can get excited about doing well in spelling, and I feel gratified to be part of the process. I hope the No Boring Practice, Please! series helps teach and inspire.

May the force be with you.

Sincerely,
Harold Jarnicki

Name _____

Syllables Have the Beat

Clap your hands and
ce-le-brate syl-la-bles!

A **syllable** is a part of a word that has one vowel sound. Every word is made up of one or more syllables.

Syllable Rules

❶ Every syllable in every word must have one vowel sound.
One vowel sound = one syllable
coat, flight, dog, gate

A **consonant digraph** is two consonants that make one sound.
th, ch, sh, ph, wh

❷ Divide between two middle consonants . . .
rab-bit, lit-tle, hap-pen
. . . BUT never split up a CONSONANT DIGRAPH.
moth-er, feath-er, graph-ite, catch-er

❸ Sometimes a syllable can be a single vowel.
o-pen, i-tem, e-vil

❹ If a syllable has a single middle vowel and a consonant on each side, divide before the first consonant.
o-pen, re-port, af-ter

❺ In words that end with a consonant plus -le (as in *syllable*), divide before the consonant preceding -le.
lit-tle, fum-ble, bub-ble
Tick-le **breaks the rule!**

❻ Divide any prefixes or suffixes.
pre-view, hope-ful, teach-er

kite
One syllable!

ap-ple
Two syllables!

It's a-bout the beat, man!

Warning! Rules work most of the time but not all the time.

syl-la-ble
Three syllables!

Sas-katch-e-wan
Four syllables!

Try it!

Divide each word into syllables and write the number of syllables. Record the rule numbers that apply to each word. See the example.

WORD	IN SYL-LA-BLES	SYLLABLES	RULES THAT APPLY
brother	broth-er	2	1, 2
riddle			
about			
disappear			
important			
communication			

The Syl-la-ble Thing

Diphthong (dif-thong) is two vowels that make one syllable.

Vowels
a, e, i, o, u

y and **w** are considered vowels when they are part of diphthongs.

ou as in *shout*

oi as in *noise*

ow as in *cow*

au as in *caught*

ou as in *bought*

oy as in *toy*

aw as in *saw*

oo as in *boot*

"Diphthong," now that's a weird word!

Try it!

Write three words for each diphthong.

ou	oi	ow	au/ou ✻	oy	aw	oo

✻ Did you know that *au*, *ou*, and *aw* can all have the same sound?

Try it!

Use the clues and unscramble the syllables to form words. Check off each syllable as you use it.

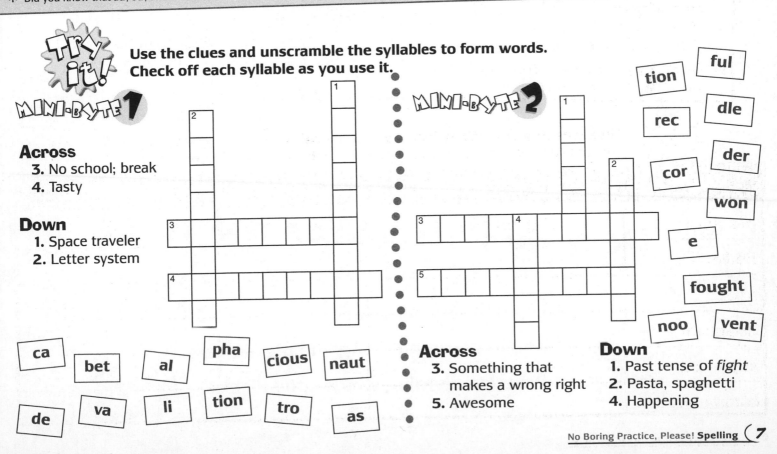

MINI-BYTE 1

Across
3. No school; break
4. Tasty

Down
1. Space traveler
2. Letter system

ca   bet   al   pha   cious   naut

de   va   li   tion   tro   as

MINI-BYTE 2

tion   ful   rec   dle   der   cor   won   e   fought   noo   vent

Across
3. Something that makes a wrong right
5. Awesome

Down
1. Past tense of *fight*
2. Pasta, spaghetti
4. Happening

MINI-BYTE 3

Across
4. Funny drawing
5. Person walking

Down
1. Think hard; focus
2. Long, long ago
3. Quiet laugh

car

an

pre

chuck

pe

ic

tri

con

des

le

toon

tor

cen

his

trate

MINI-BYTE 4

ble

le

tion

ent

te

vail

fer

za

ni

or

sion

a

a

vi

let

toi

hop

ga

dif

Across
1. Little jump
4. You can have it, if it's this
5. TV
6. Not the same

Down
2. A group or club
3. Bathroom

How do I study for the test?

Make it into a game!

Play with a friend!

- Learn the **Syllable Rules**.
- Know what **diphthong** and **digraph** are.
- **Practice dividing** words into syllables.

Name: _____

A Syllable Rules: Mark each statement as TRUE (T) or FALSE (F).

_____ **1.** Every syllable must have one vowel sound.

_____ **2.** Every syllable must have one consonant sound.

_____ **3.** Usually divide between two middle vowels.

_____ **4.** Split up a consonant digraph into two syllables.

_____ **5.** Sometimes a syllable can be a single consonant.

_____ **6.** Sometimes a syllable can be a single vowel.

_____ **7.** Divide before the consonant preceding -le, like this: un-cle.

_____ **8.** A prefix is usually a syllable on its own.

_____ **9.** Never split up one diphthong into two syllables.

_____ **10.** Usually divide between two middle consonants.

BONUS
(4 points)

Organize these syllables into a word.

| o | chol |
| gist | psy |

_____

B Definitions Score: _____ /16

1. Fill in the blanks to describe a consonant digraph.

A consonant digraph is _____ consonants making _____ sound.

2. Circle the consonant digraphs in this group: th   sk   sh   tr   ph

3. Fill in the blanks to describe a diphthong.

A diphthong is one _____ made up of two _____.

4. Circle the diphthongs in this group: uo   aw   wo   oo   oi

C Break It Down: Divide each word into syllables. Score: _____ /60

Word	In Syllables	Word	In Syllables
1. mother		**11.** astronaut	
2. cattle		**12.** adventure	
3. disappear		**13.** little	
4. communication		**14.** report	
5. frog		**15.** fought	
6. riddle		**16.** alphabet	
7. important		**17.** delicious	
8. item		**18.** invention	
9. open		**19.** noise	
10. catcher		**20.** stronger	

Name _____

The Ruler of Plurals Says...

Plural means more than one.

Follow my rules for plurals and you won't go wrong!

Plural Rule 1: Most nouns form their plurals by adding *s*.

Examples:　chair ····▶ **chairs**　　lizard ····▶ **lizards**

Change these singular nouns to plurals.

Singular	Plural	Singular	Plural
1. book		6. bank	
2. game		7. comic	
3. dream		8. pizza	
4. power		9. friend	
5. skateboard		10. graph	

Plural Rule 2: For nouns ending in *s*, *x*, *sh*, or *ch*, add *es*.

Examples:　box ····▶ **boxes**　　bush ····▶ **bushes**

Change these singular nouns to plurals.

Singular	Plural	Singular	Plural
1. kiss		6. crush	
2. fox		7. pass	
3. knish		8. tax	
4. beach		9. batch	
5. watch		10. dress	

Plural Rule 3:
For nouns that end in **y *preceded by a consonant***, change the **y** to an **i**, then add **es**.

Example: penny ·····➤ **pennies**   lady ·····➤ **ladies**

Read the story below. Then fill in the blanks using the words in the Box. But first, turn each word in the Box to plural.

THE BOX

country	city	lottery	mummy
party	celebrity	story	possibility

My Winning Tickets

This is one of my true _____. Honest! It all started when Aunt Wilma bought me three lottery tickets for my birthday. I mean, who gives a kid lottery tickets? I asked Dad to hold them for me.

Then one day, I was hanging out at home, reading about the _____ of ancient Egypt, when Dad broke the news: My ticket numbers came up in three different _____!

Suddenly, my future was filled with _____! I could travel to foreign _____. I could buy hundreds of basketballs. I could follow my favorite baseball team as they play in different _____. I could even become one of those _____ that end up on TV talk shows!

I was planning all the _____ I could throw for my friends to celebrate when Dad brought me back to reality with this reminder: You have to be 18 years old to actually win the lottery! What a bummer!

Oh well … I guess my dreams can wait a few more years.

Plural Rule 4:
Most nouns ending in **f** or **fe** can be made plural by simply adding **s**. But the plural of some nouns that end in **f** or **fe** is formed by changing the **f** to **v**, then adding **s** or **es**.

Examples: reef ·····➤ **reefs**   knife ·····➤ **knives**

Find These Words

Find the plurals for these words in the word search.

leaf	self
safe	kerchief
chief	shelf
roof	wife

```
K E R C H I E F S G S E V I W
B F R C A L E A V E S F D M I
M S Y H W I F E V U V A O F R
O P Y I P E L L M G W L W O Y
W A M E S H E L F V D Y E F R
L P Z F V S S B J M N M W H F
M S D S U N L O C T X V S U S
```

Plural Rule 5: For nouns ending in **o preceded by a vowel**, add **s**. For nouns ending in **o preceded by a consonant**, add **s** or **es**.

Examples: **radio ·····➤ radios**   **superhero ·····➤ superheroes**

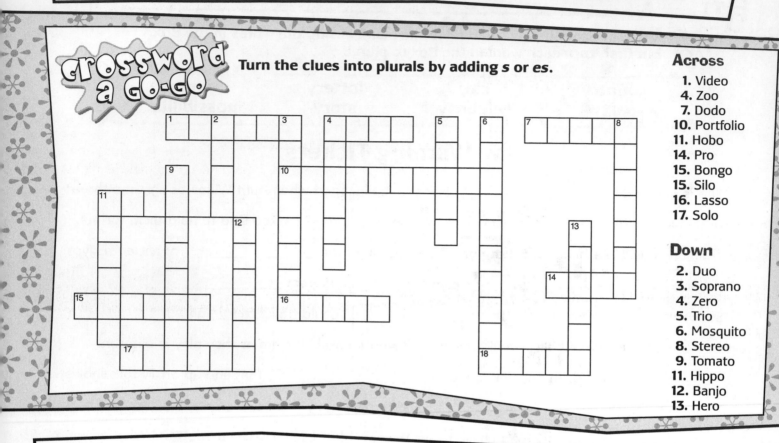

Crossword a GO-GO

Turn the clues into plurals by adding **s** or **es**.

Across
1. Video
4. Zoo
7. Dodo
10. Portfolio
11. Hobo
14. Pro
15. Bongo
15. Silo
16. Lasso
17. Solo

Down
2. Duo
3. Soprano
4. Zero
5. Trio
6. Mosquito
8. Stereo
9. Tomato
11. Hippo
12. Banjo
13. Hero

Plural Rule 6: And then there are those few nouns that don't follow any of the Plural Rules. Either the spelling of the word changes to form the plural, or the word doesn't change at all.

Example: **man ·····➤ men**   **child ·····➤ children**   **sheep ·····➤ sheep**

Plural Scramble!

Unscramble the words below. Hint: They're all plurals of the words in the singular chart.

Singular Words	
	goose
ox	woman
mouse	Chinese
tooth	salmon
deer	foot
larva	antenna

Unscramble			
		efte	
nshciee		relvaa	
nteennaa		hetet	
ciem		smonal	
onmwe		seege	
reed		noex	

Name: _____

A Plural Rules: Score: _____ /16

Mark each statement as **TRUE (T)** or **False (F)**.

_____ **1.** To pluralize all words that end in *f*, change the *f* to *v* then add *s*.

_____ **2.** Some words that form plurals don't end in *s*.

_____ **3.** Some words don't change their spelling when they become plurals.

_____ **4.** For all words that end in *o*, add *es* to change them to plurals.

_____ **5.** Words that end in *s* do not need additional letters to become plurals.

_____ **6.** If a word ends in *y* preceded by a consonant, change the *y* to *i*, then add *es* to make it plural.

_____ **7.** Adding an *s* to the end of any word makes it plural.

_____ **8.** Some words do not follow any plural rules.

BONUS
(4 points)
Write the plural of *larva*:

_____

B Plural Forms: Score: _____ /60

Spell the correct plural form of each word.

Singular	Plural	Singular	Plural
1. inch		**11.** tooth	
2. ox		**12.** deer	
3. chief		**13.** penny	
4. radio		**14.** wife	
5. potato		**15.** key	
6. woman		**16.** country	
7. goose		**17.** leaf	
8. foot		**18.** piano	
9. antenna		**19.** dish	
10. tax		**20.** Chinese	

C Find 10 Mistakes: Circle 10 plural words that are spelled   Score: _____ /20
incorrectly. Write the correct spelling on the back of this page.

Willy likes to play his bongoes in the forest to the hum of mosquitos. He loves

playing for childs, oxs, and puppys. One day Willy hopes to play his music in different

citys. Of course he will take his dancing gooses and mouses with him. He hopes to be

a big hit. His goal is to be one of the most famous bongo-playing heros ever. Until

then, he just bothers all the men and womans in the village.

Name _____

Suffix: Is This the End?

> A **suffix** is a syllable added to the end of a word to change its meaning.

Rule 1:
If a word ends with a Consonant-Vowel-Consonant, double the final consonant when adding a suffix (a.k.a. the "CVC Rule").

For example:

run	running
skip	skipped
hit	hitting

For words that don't follow the CVC Rule, just add the suffix.

For example:

jump	jumped
start	starting

Rule Breakers! These words break **Rule 1**.

edit	edited
carpet	carpeting
judge	judgment

Rule 2:
If a word ends in e, drop the e, then add the suffix. If the suffix is -ed, just add -d.

For example:

dance	dancing	danced
race	racing	raced

BUT if the suffix begins with a consonant like -ly or -ment, leave the e on.

For example:

love	lovely
place	placement

Rule Breakers! These words break **Rule 2**.

true	truly
argue	argument
judge	judgment

> As the Royal Dude of Spelling, I command thee to make thy spelling better!

 Try it!

Follow the examples and fill in the charts.

WORD	ADD -ing	ADD -ed	WORD	ADD -ing	ADD -ment, -ly, or -ful
flip	flipping	flipped	hope	hoping	hopeful
ram			place		
fit			care		
sort			shape		
camp			arrange		
act			move		

Rule 3:

If a word ends in a consonant plus *y* (as in *fry*), change the *y* to *i* and add any suffix that doesn't begin with *i*.

Here the rule works perfectly!

For example:

| try | trying | tried | tries |

The word *key* ends in *y*, but a consonant doesn't come before the *y*. So here the rule does not work perfectly.

Pay attention:

| key | keying | keyed | keys |

Try it!

Follow the examples and fill in the charts.

WORD	ADD -ing	ADD -ed	ADD -s
marry	marrying	married	marries
carry			
bury			
ferry			
play			

Spell It! Spell these words correctly.

❶ happy + ness = _____

❷ plenty + ful = _____

❸ satisfy + s = _____

❹ healthy + ness = _____

❺ pity + less = _____

❻ beauty + ful = _____

❼ hurry + ed = _____

❽ party + s = _____

❾ merry + ment = _____

❿ funny + er = _____

Correct It! Write the correct form of the word on the line.

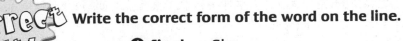

That's so cool!

❶ **final**   She _____ finished eating her broccoli.

❷ **appear** We saw a flash, then all of a sudden, a ghost _____!

❸ **beauty** Those flowers are _____.

❹ **plan**   We _____ to go to the movies yesterday.

❺ **happy**   _____ is a bowl full of chocolate.

Groovy Suffix X-WORD

Combine each word and suffix to complete the puzzle.

I think this is doable!

Across

5. hope + ing
7. true + ly
8. open + ed
10. win + ing
11. change + able
13. prepare + ing
14. rob + ery
15. shape + ing
16. final + ly

17. control + er
20. slide + ing
23. do + ing
24. carpet + ing
25. edit + ed
26. achieve + ment
27. scoop + ing
28. write + ing

Down

1. achieve + ing
2. dive + ing
3. stubborn + ness
4. fly + ing
6. recreate + tion
9. nine + ty
11. change + ing
12. arrange + ment
13. plan + ed

18. fan + ed
19. judge + ment
21. lose + ing
22. hop + ing

Name: _____

A Correction!
Circle each misspelled word. Then spell the words correctly on the lines below.

Score: _____ /24

openned   lovely   sitting   arrangeing   trys   monkeys   beautyful   famus
robery   swimming   appearance   hurryed   campper   arguement   truely
planner   finaly   skating   satisfied   skipping   funnier   actting

Correct it here:

1.	5.	9.
2.	6.	10.
3.	7.	11.
4.	8.	12.

B Change It!
Spell each form of the word correctly.

Score: _____ /24

WORD	ADD -ing	ADD -ed
1. flip		
2. place		
3. move		
4. appear		
5. hurry		
6. play		
7. control		
8. edit		

BONUS
(12 points)
Sound out this word and spell it correctly:
beeyootifikashun
_____

C Spell It Out:
Combine the words and suffixes below. Spell the words correctly.

Score: _____ /40

1. happy + ness	**11.** lose + ing
2. prepare + ing	**12.** achieve + ment
3. recreate + tion	**13.** plenty + ful
4. fly + ing	**14.** fan + ed
5. die + ing	**15.** scoop + ing
6. beauty + fy	**16.** healthy + ness
7. carpet + ed	**17.** chop + ed
8. judge + ment	**18.** move + ment
9. dive + s	**19.** sky + s
10. nine + ty	**20.** carry + er

The Silent Letters

Quiet, please!

Some letters in words can be quite sneaky. They don't make any sound at all. Check out these **silent letters**.

Silent D		Silent T		Silent L	
Wednesday	hedge	witch	fasten	palm	talk
handsome	wedge	watch	castle	calm	walk
handkerchief		scratch	listen	salmon	folk
badge		match		calf	yolk
edge		butcher		half	almond

Use the words on the chart to fill in the blanks below.

❶ Write three Silent D words that rhyme with each other.

_____ _____ _____

❷ Write two Silent T words that rhyme with each other.

_____ _____

❸ From the Silent L words, write the rhyming:

"lm" words: _____ _____

"lf" words: _____ _____

"alk" words: _____ _____

"olk" words: _____ _____

❹ Write the Silent D word that has three syllables. Put a hyphen between each syllable.

_____

❺ Write four Silent T words that have two syllables. Put a hyphen between each syllable.

_____ _____

_____ _____

❻ Write two Silent L words that have two syllables. Put a hyphen between each syllable.

_____ _____

Silent Word Chart

Silent K		Silent G		Silent B	
knife	know	gnaw	design	thumb	climbing
knee	knew	gnu	foreigner	numb	bomb
knot	knob	sign		crumb	comb
knit	knock			lamb	doubt

Use the words on the chart to fill in the blanks below.

❶ Give a Silent K word for each definition.

Past tense of *know*: _____

You tie it: _____

Helps you open a door: _____

Leg joint: _____

Used to slice bread: _____

❷ In the chart, all Silent K's and Silent G's are followed by what letter? _____

❸ Give a Silent G word for each definition.

Person from another country: _____

A pattern: _____

Type of antelope: _____

To chew on: _____

A symbol: _____

> Do you know what a gnu is? No doubt you'll find the answer on this page.

❹ Most Silent B's follow what letter? _____

The only word in our list that breaks this rule is _____

❺ Write three rhyming Silent B words: _____ _____

_____

❻ Write the correct spelling for each of these phonetically spelled words.

kohm: _____   **bom:** _____

lam: _____   **kliming:** _____

silent word chart

Silent H		Silent W		Silent U	
what	where	write	wrong	guest	guilty
when	honest	wrestling	wrist	guess	league
why	hour	wrinkle	wrote	guitar	tongue
which	ghost	whole	two	guard	biscuit
		wreck	sword	building	
		wrapper			

Use the words on the chart to fill in the blanks below.

❶ Which Silent H words are often used in questions?

_____ _____ _____

_____ _____

❷ Write three Silent H words (other than *honest*) that begin with "hon-." **Hint:** A dictionary may help.

_____ _____ _____

❸ Boo! What's this Silent H word? _____

❹ What two Silent W words don't begin with *w*. _____ _____

❺ Silent W word clues:

Past tense of *write*: _____

What a smashed-up car might be called: _____

Attaches hand to arm: _____

All of something: _____

Use an iron to get rid of this: _____

Not right: _____

Covers a present: _____

I honestly can't guess which guest is in the wrestling league.

Shh. . . Someone might hear you!

❻ Most silent U's follow what letter? _____

Write all the words that follow this rule. _____

_____ _____

_____ _____

Name: _____

Score: _____ /100

Sound It Out: Sound out these phonetically spelled words and spell them correctly.

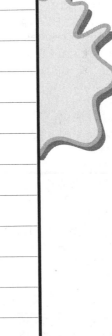

Phonetic Spelling	Correct Spelling
1. majik	
2. peess	
3. byesikuhl	
4. jyeuhnt	
5. seyeklaups	
6. jimnayzeeuhm	
7. syeklone	
8. ayjuhnt	
9. eksite	
10. syeuhnss	
11. spuhnj	
12. guhrahj	
13. seeling	
14. jyerate	
15. kneess	
16. lounj	
17. enjuhn	
18. juhj	
19. suhlebruhtee	
20. surkuhl	
21. jentuhl	
22. meduhsuhn	
23. orinj	
24. diside	
25. trajik	

Fun with PH

PH = F sound

pharmacy   phony   graph

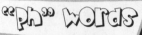

Match It!

Match each "ph" word below with its correct meaning.

"Ph" words

morph
phobia
phenomenon
bibliography
geography
photograph
telephone
pharmacy
Philadelphia
biography
graph
pharaoh
phony
phase
phrase
physical

Meanings

Egyptian ruler
fake
of a material thing
drugstore
stage of development
fear
a few words together
list of books
life story
to change to another form
camera picture
an exceptional thing or event
study of Earth's physical features
diagram that shows data
communication device
city in Pennsylvania

We don't have words like these in our planet!

Hint: Use the dictionary.

He's definitely got a "ph" phobia.

"Ph" word search!

Circle 20 "ph" words in this word search.

```
A M H K N P R A N K Z L A C I S Y H P Y
I Y P W H R J I Y M G E L H P F M L H H
H H A V Y O Y B M K G W P K P Y R H E P
P P R J M P C O Y R H R M H P M Y N N A
L A G J L H X H H O P A N P B M N O R G
E R O L Z E P P D M P N H H C Z J M G G
D G T K K T D H H N T A R A C P T Z E O
A O O R B D X P O O Y A R L R C M E N I
L E H K N R A Z M N S H Q G N M S Y O L
I G P Q X R N N M E Y V J K O A A C N B
H L Q W G T E L E P H O N E H I L C B I
P H A R A O H P M W B L B P M N B Z Y B
```

Name _____

Fill in the blanks with the correct "ph" word.

What's the PH word?

morph	pharmacy	phase
arachnophobia	Philadelphia	phantom
phenomenon	biography	phrase
bibliography	graph	physical
geography	pharaohs	nymph
photograph	phony	telephone

1. I read Martin Luther King Jr's _____ to learn about his life.

2. She has _____—she's afraid of spiders.

3. Please repeat that _____. I couldn't hear you.

4. Mr. Go went to the _____ to buy some aspirin.

5. _____ activity will make you strong.

6. The solar eclipse was quite a _____!

7. These pictures will look great in my _____ album.

8. Our teacher made us include a _____ with our project.

9. Let's chart our answers using a bar _____.

10. Just be yourself. Don't be _____.

11. _____ is a big city in Pennsylvania.

12. A dragonfly larva is called a _____.

13. Mom says my teenage sister is going through a _____.

14. Sorry I didn't call you. Our _____ was out of order.

15. Watch out for the _____ ghost from the green lagoon!

16. The _____ of Egypt were buried with most of their riches.

17. That cow can _____ into a three-eyed monster!

18. In _____ class, we learn about our country.

Name: _____

Score: _____ /54

A Spell Correctly:

Write the correct spelling of each of these phonetically spelled **"ph"** words.

Phonetic Spelling	Correct Spelling	Phonetic Spelling	Correct Spelling
1. bibleeogruhfee		10. fohbeeuh	
2. byeogruhfee		11. fohtuhgraf	
3. fairoh		12. fonee	
4. fantuhm		13. fraze	
5. farmuhsee		14. graf	
6. faze		15. jeeogruhfee	
7. fenomuhnon		16. morf	
8. filedelfea		17. nimf	
9. fizuhkuhl		18. teluhfone	

B Fill It In: Write the most appropriate **"ph"** word in the blank.

Score: _____ /30

1. In this _____ everyone is smiling.

2. King Tut was one of the most famous _____ of ancient Egypt.

3. A tadpole goes through more than one _____ to become a frog.

4. The _____ is ringing! Please answer it.

5. The baby genius is a _____.

6. Dad's story about the ghostly _____ wasn't scary.

7. When I saw our cat _____ into a dog, I knew it was time to run.

8. We studied the _____ of South America.

9. That list of books makes a good _____.

10. I had to wait in line at the _____ for my grandma's medicine.

BONUS
(16 points)

What do you call the fear of open places?

_____

Commonly Confused Words

Some words sound alike, but
they are not spelled alike.

Round 1

Commonly confused

Fill in the blanks with the correct word.

TO: helps indicate a direction; connection to something
Let's go _to_ the Sponge Boys concert.
We all began _to_ sing.

TOO: more than enough; also
That's _too_ much ice cream.
Graham is coming, _too_.

TWO: spelling for number 2
Sonya has _two_ goldfish.

THERE: at that place
Meet me over _there_.

THEIR: belonging to them
Joe's cousins like _their_ new house.

THEY'RE: contraction for "they are"
They're good storywriters.

YOUR: belonging to you
Thanks for letting me borrow _your_ bike.

YOU'RE: contraction for "you are"
You're my best friend.

ITS: belonging to it
The bird built _its_ nest in the tree.

IT'S: contraction for "it is"
_It's_ a lovely day.

1. I want _____ go _____.

2. _____ of you can sit in front.

3. _____ is _____ many
_____ ride on one bike.

4. _____ house is over _____.

5. _____ going to meet us later.

6. _____ in the bushes, _____ hiding.

7. _____ supposed to wait with me.

8. _____ flowers are growing!

9. _____ mom wants you to come as
soon as _____ finished.

10. _____ going to rain tonight.

11. The dog gobbled down _____ dinner.

12. If _____ too cold, I will stay in.

Commonly Confused Words

Round 2

Commonly Confused

ALREADY: by this time
We did that *already*.

ALL READY: prepared to do something
We're *all ready* to go.

RIGHT: correct; opposite of left; part of immediately
Jordy's work is *right*.
Turn *right* at the corner.
Come here *right* away.

WRITE: mark down (on paper)
I want to *write* a story.

WEAR: to have on
She's going to *wear* her soccer jersey.

WHERE: in what place
Where are you going?

THREW: past tense of *throw*
The catcher *threw* to second base.

THROUGH: in one side and out the other; finished
I had to climb *through* the window.
I'm all *through* with work.

THAN: used mainly in comparisons
Irvin is older *than* Katharine.

THEN: means "at that time" or "soon after"
We went to the park, and *then* we played tag.

Fill in the blanks with the correct word.

1. She is _____ to leave.

2. We have been _____ since morning.

3. I _____ finished.

4. Are you _____? Let's go!

5. _____ that in your book.

6. That was the _____ thing to do.

7. _____ that in the _____ hand corner of the paper.

8. Do it _____ now!

9. _____ is the party?

10. I don't know _____ to put that.

11. Are you going to _____ the red hat?

12. _____ your swimsuit to the park.

13. I _____ the garbage into the can.

14. Can you get _____ the maze?

15. Put the thread _____ the eye of the needle.

16. I _____ the ball as hard as I could.

17. Until _____, she had never laughed.

18. Run, _____ walk.

19. I'd rather read _____ dig that hole.

20. She's looking better _____ ever!

Commonly Confused Words

Round 3

Commonly confused

Fill in the blanks with the correct word.

WHOLE: all of it
   I ate the *whole* pie myself.

HOLE: an empty place
   Don't fall into that deep *hole*.

1. We need to dig a _____.

2. I have to complete the _____ thing.

3. Watch out for the _____ there.

4. The _____ team will be at the game.

BREAK: come apart; no longer work; space
   If you *break* the lock, we won't get in.
   Give me a *break*!

BRAKE: stop; stopping device
   Brake at the red light.

5. Let's take a ten-minute _____.

6. Step on the _____.

7. _____ before you hit the fence.

8. Don't drop the dish or it will _____.

NO: negative
   There's *no* way I'm going.

KNOW: to understand or be aware of
   I *know* the answer.

9. _____, I think I'll stay home.

10. Does he _____ your name?

11. My dad will _____ the way.

12. There was _____ one there.

NEW: just purchased or made
   The *new* car shone in the sun.

KNEW: past tense of *know*
   I *knew* that yesterday.

13. Jojo _____ you were coming.

14. I _____ the answer, but I have forgotten it.

15. We're moving into our _____ house.

PIECE: a part of
   Please give her a big *piece* of pie.

PEACE: calm
   I could feel *peace* out in the woods.

16. Can I please have a _____ of that?

17. He is having another _____.

18. Let's have _____, not war!

Commonly Confused Words
Round 4

Commonly confused

WEATHER: atmospheric conditions
   The *weather* is so hot and humid.

WHETHER: if it happens that
   I am not sure *whether* we are going or not.

ACCEPT: receive or agree with
   I want you to *accept* this award.
   Do you *accept* my idea?

EXCEPT: not including
   He likes them all *except* for the blue one.

HERE: in this place
   I'm *here* hiding in the bushes.

HEAR: sense through the ear (auditory)
   Can you *hear* the waterfall?

PLANE: aircraft
   We traveled over the mountains by *plane*.

PLAIN: simple, not fancy
   I'll wear a *plain* dress to the concert.

PAST: before now
   In the museum, we see cool things from the *past*.

PASSED: went by; advanced; handed to
   Faster cars *passed* the slow one.
   Sally *passed* into grade six!
   Bob *passed* her the ball.

Fill in the blanks with the correct word.

1. Pam is going _____ you go or not.

2. It's been lovely _____ this summer.

3. He's not sure _____ he can attend.

4. We'll check the _____ before going.

5. I can go every day _____ Monday.

6. Sam won't _____ her present.

7. _____ me as I am.

8. He'll eat any vegetable _____ beans.

9. I can _____ all the instruments.

10. Come _____ now!

11. _____ we go again.

12. Please _____ what I have to say.

13. I'll just have my pizza _____ this time.

14. She is just a _____ dog , but we love her.

15. Everything looked so tiny from the _____.

16. It's just _____ old me!

17. Grandpa likes to talk about the _____.

18. We all _____ the drivers' course.

19. She _____ me when we raced.

20. It's hard to remember some things about my

   _____.

Name _____

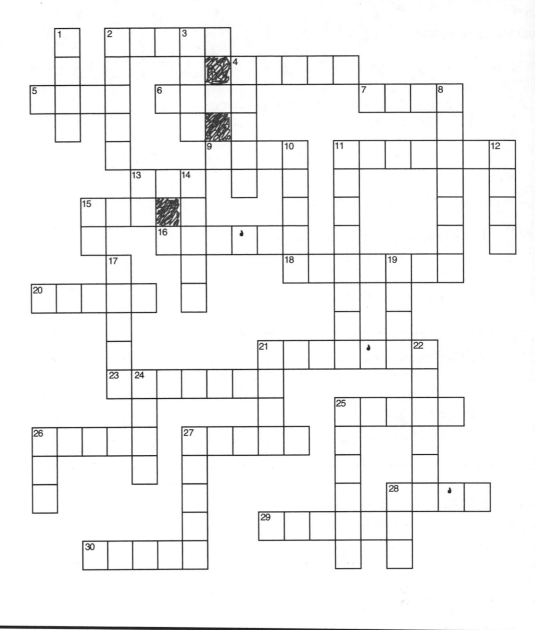

I'm all ready two confused too no weather or not my answers are write.

Across
2. Mark down on paper
4. Stop! Hit the _____!
5. You dig it
6. To have on
7. Past tense of *know*
9. Before now
11. By this time
13. Not old
15. 1 + 1
16. You are
18. If it happens that
20. Not fancy
21. They are
23. In one end and out the other
25. Calm and quiet
26. Belonging to them
27. Aircraft
28. It is
29. Receive
30. At that place

Down
1. To understand or be aware of
2. In what place?
3. Soon after
4. To make into pieces
8. Atmospheric conditions
10. Past tense of *throw*
11. Prepared to do something
12. Belonging to you
13. Negative response
14. All of it
15. Indicates direction or connection
17. Correct
19. Sense through ears
21. Used to compare
22. Not including
24. In this place
25. Went by
26. Also
27. A part of
28. Belonging to it

QUICKIE QUIZ Commonly Confused Words

Survivor Challenge

Fill in the blanks with the Commonly Confused Words in Rounds 1 to 4. **Hint:** Keep the worksheets from Rounds 1 to 4 handy.

My Island Holiday

_____ not a story that is easy to tell, but I'll try _____ explain the _____ thing.

I hopped into my private _____ at the _____ of dawn. With a cloudless sky, the _____ was perfect. I had been _____ stressed for weeks. I was really looking forward _____ some _____ and quiet far, far away from civilization.

I had been in the air for about _____ hours before I _____ something was wrong—very wrong. I could _____ one engine cough and sputter. One of my engines stopped working. I tried to see _____ the other one was going _____. I took a quick look below me and saw an island. I would have _____ fly _____ the trees and make an emergency landing on the beach. I flew _____ some coconut trees, knocking _____ coconuts _____ the ground. I was concentrating hard and managed _____ touch down and stop without a problem. "At least _____ I'm safe," I said out loud.

I heard some branches snapping. I looked left. I looked _____. I couldn't see anything. My heart started beating faster. I was just happy to be _____, safe on the ground, but I was worried. I _____ something or someone was watching me. I grabbed a branch and began to _____ H-E-L-P in the sand.

_____ was that sound again. This time I saw _____ it came from. I decided to investigate.

I walked _____ my _____ and into the jungle. I could tell that someone had just run _____. I kept walking in the same direction. Suddenly I found myself in a clearing surrounded by people and cameras.

"_____ about time you got _____" a woman with an English accent said. "We've had everything _____ and waiting for you for an hour. What took you so long?"

"This is all _____ confusing," I said. "_____ am I? Who are you?"

"_____ on Bogo-Bogo Island! _____ the newest winner of a million dollars!"

Answer Key

Syllables Have the Beat! (p. 6)

Word	In Syl-la-bles	Number of Syllables	Rules That Apply
brother	broth-er	2	1, 2
riddle	rid-dle	2	1, 2, 5
about	a-bout	2	1, 3
disappear	dis-ap-pear	3	1, 2, 6
important	im-por-tant	3	1, 4, 6
communication	com-mu-ni-ca-tion	5	1, 2, 4, 6

The Syllable Thing (pp. 7–8)
Answers may vary, but could include:
- **ou** – out, about, snout, pout
- **oi** – oil, toil, boil, soil
- **ow** – now, bow, brow, chow
- **au/ou** – taught, astronaut, fought, thought
- **oy** – boy, decoy, Roy, annoy
- **aw** – paw, law, claw, draw
- **oo** – shoot, toot, loot, root

Mini-Byte 1
Mini-Byte 2
Mini-Byte 3
Mini-Byte 4

Quickie Quiz: Syllables (p. 9)
Syllable Rules:

1. T	3. F	5. F	7. T	9. T
2. F	4. F	6. T	8. T	10. T

BONUS: psychologist

Definitions:
1. two, one
2. th, sh, ph
3. sound, vowels
4. aw, oo, oi

Break It Down:
1. moth-er
2. cat-tle
3. dis-ap-pear
4. com-mu-ni-ca-tion
5. frog
6. rid-dle
7. im-por-tant
8. i-tem
9. o-pen
10. catch-er
11. as-tro-naut
12. ad-ven-ture
13. lit-tle
14. re-port
15. fought
16. al-pha-bet
17. de-li-cious
18. in-ven-tion
19. noise
20. strong-er

The Ruler of Plural Says... (pp. 10–12)
Try it!

1. books
2. games
3. dreams
4. powers
5. skateboards
6. banks
7. comics
8. pizzas
9. friends
10. graphs

1. kisses
2. foxes
3. knishes
4. beaches
5. watches
6. crushes
7. passes
8. taxes
9. batches
10. dresses

Fill Me In
stories; mummies; lotteries; possibilities; countries; cities; celebrities; parties

Find Those Words

Crossword a Go-Go

Plural Scramble
Chinese
antennae
mice
women
deer
feet
larvae
teeth
salmon
geese
oxen

Quickie Quiz: Plurals (p. 13)
Plural Rules

1. F	3. T	5. F	7. F
2. T	4. F	6. T	8. T

BONUS: larvae

Plural Forms
1. inches
2. oxen
3. chiefs
4. radios
5. potatoes
6. women
7. geese
8. feet
9. antennae
10. taxes
11. teeth
12. deer
13. pennies
14. wives
15. keys
16. countries
17. leaves
18. pianos
19. dishes
20. Chinese

Find 10 Mistakes
bongos; mosquitoes; children; oxen; puppies; cities; geese; mice; heroes; women

Suffix: Is This the End? (pp. 14–15)
Rule 1 and Rule 2: Try It!

Word	ADD -ing	ADD -ed
ram	ramming	rammed
fit	fitting	fitted
sort	sorting	sorted
camp	camping	camped
act	acting	acted
hope	hoping	hopeful/hopefully
place	placing	placement
care	caring	careful/carefully
shape	shaping	shapely
arrange	arranging	arrangement
move	moving	movement

Rule 3: Try It!

Word	ADD -ing	ADD -ed	ADD -s
carry	carrying	carried	carries
bury	burying	buried	buries
ferry	ferrying	ferried	ferries
play	playing	played	plays

Spell It!
1. happiness 3. satisfies 5. pitiless 7. hurried 9. merriment
2. plentiful 4. healthiness 6. beautiful 8. parties 10. funnier

Correct It!
1. finally 3. beautiful 5. Happiness
2. appeared 4. planned

Groovy Suffix X-word (p. 16)

Quickie Quiz: Suffix (p. 17)

Correction!
1. opened 5. famous 9. argument
2. arranging 6. robbery 10. truly
3. tries 7. hurried 11. finally
4. beautiful 8. camper 12. acting

Change It!
1. flip — flipping — flipped
2. place — placing — placed
3. move — moving — moved
4. appear — appearing — appeared
5. hurry — hurrying — hurried
6. play — playing — played
7. control — controlling — controlled
8. edit — editing — edited

BONUS: beautification

Spell It Out!
1. happiness 6. beautify 11. losing 16. healthiness
2. preparing 7. carpeted 12. achievement 17. chopped
3. recreation 8. judgment 13. plentiful 18. movement
4. flying 9. dives 14. fanned 19. skies
5. dying 10. ninety 15. scooping 20. carrier

The Silent Letter (pp. 18–20)

Let's Do It! (p. 18)
1. edge, hedge, wedge
2. watch, scratch, match
3. palm, calm; calf, half; talk, walk; folk, yolk
4. hand-ker-chief
5. butch-er, fas-ten, cas-tle, lis-ten
6. salm-on, al-mond

Let's Do It! (p. 19)
1. knew, knot, knob, knee, knife
2. n
3. foreigner, design, gnu, gnaw, sign
4. m; doubt
5. thumb, numb, crumb
6. comb, lamb, bomb, climbing

Let's Do It! (p. 20)
1. what, when, why, which, where
2. Answers may vary, but could include: honesty, honor, honorable
3. ghost
4. two, sword
5. wrote, wreck, wrist, whole, wrinkle, wrong, wrapper
6. g; guest, guess, guitar, guard, guilty, league, tongue

Silent Letter Mega Crossword (p. 21)

Unscramble
1. hour 4. wrong, grown 7. match
2. knew 5. lamb 8. knife
3. ghost 6. doubt 9. listen

Quickie Quiz: Silent Letters (p. 22)

1. Wednesday 8. crumb 15. Guard 22. knit
2. Listen 9. know 16. wrestling 23. Half
3. chalk 10. doubt 17. building 24. walk
4. yolk 11. tongue 18. guitar
5. knee 12. ghost 19. two
6. Climbing 13. league 20. biscuits
7. design 14. write 21. foreigner

BONUS: amond

AU ... It's Painless! (p. 23)

Fill 'em Up!
1. nauseous 3. daughter 5. cautious 7. applause
2. cause 4. sauce 6. haunted 8. astronaut

Rule Breakers
1. b 2. c 3. c

Word Search

fought
sought
bought
brought
thought

Quickie Quiz: AU Words (p. 24)
What's Right?
1. d   3. a   5. a   7. d
2. a   4. b   6. c   8. b

BONUS: because

Correct It!
1. bought   3. sauce   5. haunted   7. aunt
2. thought   4. laughed 6. nauseous   8. caught

EI … IE … Oh! (p. 25)
Try It!
1. sleigh (2)   3. cashier (1)   5. veil (2)   7. Either (3)
2. thief (1)   4. receipt (1)   6. counterfeit (2) 8. shriek (1)

Groovy EI…IE X-word (p. 26)

Crossword grid with answers: FIELD, SCENT, COUNTER, FIGHTING, REIGN, HEIGHT, BELIEVE, CASHIER, SHRIEK, CHIEF, VEIL, RECEIVE, CONCEITED, GRIEF, CEILING, HOIST, GLORY, YIELD, MISCHIEF, THIEF, WEIRD, PRIEST, PERCEIVE, SEIZURE, FRIEND, SLEIGH, NEIGH, FREIGHT

Quickie Quiz: EI…IE Words (p. 27)
What's Right?
1. c   3. b   5. d   7. d   9. a
2. c   4. c   6. a   8. d   10. b

Sound Out & Spell
1. veil   5. eight   9. grief   13. mischief
2. either   6. believe   10. freight 14. priest
3. counterfeit   7. conscience 11. weight 15. leisure
4. friend   8. conceited 12. niece

BONUS: seize

The IGH Thing (p. 28)
Rap It Up!
Answers may vary; possible answers could be: right; night; flight; right; bright light; fight; knight; tight; right; bright light; might; fright; plight; bright light; bright light

Mix & Match
highlight   headlight   uptight   midnight
moonlight   tonight   eyesight   playwright

The I's Have It! (p. 29)

Crossword grid with answers: FAHRENHEIT, KITE, WHITE, PARASITE, DYNAMITE, BITE, HEIGHT, SATELLITE

Editor Dude
1. midnight   3. bright   5. Fahrenheit   7. might   9. high
2. fright   4. dynamite   6. tight   8. light   10. height

Quickie Quiz: I-IGH Words (p. 30)
Spell It Correctly
1. flight   6. kite   11. satellite   16. fright
2. knight   7. parasite   12. height   17. tight
3. fight   8. Fahrenheit   13. headlight   18. might
4. bright   9. white   14. night   19. high
5. light   10. right, write 15. dynamite   20. highlight

What's the Word?
1. height   3. parasite   5. sight
2. dynamite   4. satellite

BONUS: megabyte

The TION and SION Show (p. 31)
Fill 'em Up!
1. explosion   4. competition   7. lotion   10. population
2. subtraction   5. edition   8. vision   11. conclusion
3. preparation   6. decision   9. station   12. fraction

Syllable Scramble
1. multiplication   3. relation   5. illusion
2. conversation   4. incision   6. invasion

Quickie Quiz: -TION and -SION (p. 32)
Find 20 Mistakes
1. Nation   6. Conversation   11. perspiration   16. salutation
2. illusion   7. competition   12. explosion   17. interruption
3. multiplication   8. preparation   13. precipitation   18. situation
4. precipitation   9. attention   14. invasion   19. subtraction
5. frustration   10. confusion   15. conclusion   20. hesitation

Soft G and C (p. 33)
Soft G and C Word Search

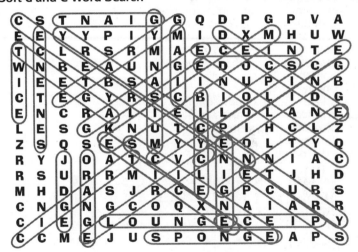

Tongue Twisters! (p. 34)
Answers will vary.

Soft G and C X-word

Quickie Quiz: Soft G and C (p. 35)
Sound It Out

1. magic	8. agent	15. niece	22. medicine
2. piece	9. excite	16. lounge	23. orange
3. bicycle	10. science	17. engine	24. decide
4. giant	11. sponge	18. judge	25. tragic
5. cyclops	12. garage	19. celebrity	
6. gymnasium	13. ceiling	20. circle	
7. cyclone	14. gyrate	21. gentle	

Fun With PH (p. 36)
Match It!

morph – to change to another form
phobia – fear
phenomenon – an exceptional thing or event
bibliography – a list of books
geography – study of Earth's physical features
photograph – camera picture
telephone – communication device
pharmacy – drugstore
Philadelphia – city in Pennsylvania
biography – life story
graph – diagram that shows data
pharaoh – Egyptian ruler
phony – fake
phase – stage of development
phrase – a few words together
physical – of a material thing

PH Word Search

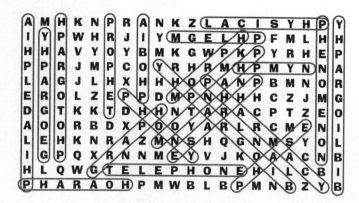

What's the PH Word? (p. 37)

1. biography	6. phenomenon	11. Philadelphia	16. pharaohs
2. arachnophobia	7. photograph	12. nymph	17. morph
3. phrase	8. bibliography	13. phase	18. geography
4. pharmacy	9. graph	14. telephone	
5. Physical	10. phony	15. phantom	

Quickie Quiz: PH Words (p. 38)
Spell Correctly

1. bibliography	10. phobia
2. biography	11. photograph
3. pharaoh	12. phony
4. phantom	13. phrase
5. pharmacy	14. graph
6. phase	15. geography
7. phenomenon	16. morph
8. Philadelphia	17. nymph
9. physical	18. telephone

Fill It In

1. photograph	4. telephone	7. morph	10. pharmacy
2. pharaohs	5. phenomenon	8. geography	
3. phase	6. phantom	9. bibliography	

Bonus: agoraphobia

Commonly Confused Words (pp. 39–42)
Round 1 (p. 39)

1. to, too	5. They're	9. Your, you're
2. Two	6. There, they're	10. It's
3. Two, too, to	7. You're	11. its
4. Their, there	8. Your	12. it's

Round 2 (p. 40)

1. all ready	6. right	11. wear	16. threw
2. all ready	7. Write, right	12. Wear	17. then
3. already	8. right	13. threw	18. then
4. all ready	9. Where	14. through	19. than
5. Write	10. where	15. through	20. than

Round 3 (p. 41)

1. hole	6. brake	11. know	16. piece
2. whole	7. Brake	12. no	17. piece
3. hole	8. break	13. knew	18. peace
4. whole	9. No	14. knew	
5. break	10. know	15. new	

Round 4 (p. 42)

1. whether	6. accept	11. Here	16. plain
2. weather	7. Accept	12. hear	17. past
3. whether	8. except	13. plain	18. passed
4. weather	9. hear	14. plain	19. passed
5. except	10. here	15. plane	20. past

Commonly Confused Crossword (p. 43)

Quickie Quiz: Confused Words (p. 44)

It's; to; whole; plane; break; weather; too; to; peace; two; knew;
hear; whether; too; to; through; past; two; to; to; here; right;
there; knew; write; There; where; past; plane; through; It's; here;
all ready; too; Where; You're; You're